PERSONAL INFORMATION

Name:	Date of Birth:

Address:

Mobile Telephone:

Home Telephone:

Email:

Blood Group:

Weight:

Height:

EMERGENCY CONTACT

Name:	Relationship:

Address:

Mobile Telephone:

Home Telephone:

Email:

INSTRUCTIONS

Keeping track of your espenses, profit, and loses are an integral part of running a successfuk business.

These sheets are a quick and easy system to keep track of how yourbusiness is doing, and record daily sales.

KEEPING AN EYE ON YOUR PROFIT AND LOSS WILL HELP YOU :

.Identify where and when you need to improve.
.Which items bring the most profit, sell more of those.
.Which items the less profit, avoid these.

HERE ARE SOME POINTS:

.Have a calculator on hand to compute your fees to be exact.
.Use self-adhesive tabs to mark the pafe your are on.
.**Sold Price:** Price your itel sold without shipping.
.**Shipping:** How much you charged for shipping.
.**Total Price:** Add Sold Price + Shipping.
.**COGS:** Cost of Goods Sold. How much you paid for your item.
.**Shipping:** How much was the actual shipping cost.
.**eBay fees:** at printing time, overall eBay fee for most categories is 11.50% of the total Price (Price + shipping).
.**Total Cost:** COGS +Actual Shipping Cost + eBay fees.
.**Profit or Loss:** Total Price – (minus) Total Cost.

STORE NAME: _____   MONTH: _____   YEAR _____

EBAY DAILY SALES TRACKERS

DATE	ITEM	SOLD PRICE	SHIPPING	TOTAL PRICE	COGS	SHIPPING	EBAY FEES	TOTAL COST	PROFIT/ LOSS

STORE NAME: _____ MONTH: _____ YEAR _____

EBAY DAILY SALES TRACKERS

DATE	ITEM	SOLD PRICE	SHIPPING	TOTAL PRICE	COGS	SHIPPING	EBAY FEES	TOTAL COST	PROFIT/ LOSS

STORE NAME: _____ MONTH: _____ YEAR _____

EBAY DAILY SALES TRACKERS

DATE	ITEM	SOLD PRICE	SHIPPING	TOTAL PRICE	COGS	SHIPPING	EBAY FEES	TOTAL COST	PROFIT/ LOSS

STORE NAME: _____ MONTH: _____ YEAR: _____

EBAY DAILY SALES TRACKERS

DATE	ITEM	SOLD PRICE	SHIPPING	TOTAL PRICE	COGS	SHIPPING	EBAY FEES	TOTAL COST	PROFIT/ LOSS

STORE NAME: _____ MONTH: _____ YEAR _____

EBAY DAILY SALES TRACKERS

DATE	ITEM	SOLD PRICE	SHIPPING	TOTAL PRICE	COGS	SHIPPING	EBAY FEES	TOTAL COST	PROFIT/ LOSS

EBAY DAILY SALES TRACKERS

STORE NAME: _____ MONTH: _____ YEAR _____

DATE	ITEM	SOLD PRICE	SHIPPING	TOTAL PRICE	COGS	SHIPPING	EBAY FEES	TOTAL COST	PROFIT/ LOSS

STORE NAME: _____   MONTH: _____   YEAR _____

DATE	ITEM	SOLD PRICE	SHIPPING	TOTAL PRICE	COGS	SHIPPING	EBAY FEES	TOTAL COST	PROFIT/ LOSS

STORE NAME: _____ MONTH: _____ YEAR _____ EBAY DAILY SALES TRACKERS

DATE	ITEM	SOLD PRICE	SHIPPING	TOTAL PRICE	COGS	SHIPPING	EBAY FEES	TOTAL COST	PROFIT/ LOSS

STORE NAME: _____ MONTH: _____ YEAR _____

EBAY DAILY SALES TRACKERS

DATE	ITEM	SOLD PRICE	SHIPPING	TOTAL PRICE	COGS	SHIPPING	EBAY FEES	TOTAL COST	PROFIT/ LOSS

STORE NAME: _____   MONTH: _____   YEAR _____

DATE	ITEM	SOLD PRICE	SHIPPING	TOTAL PRICE	COGS	SHIPPING	EBAY FEES	TOTAL COST	PROFIT/ LOSS

STORE NAME: _____ MONTH: _____ YEAR _____

EBAY DAILY SALES TRACKERS

DATE	ITEM	SOLD PRICE	SHIPPING	TOTAL PRICE	COGS	SHIPPING	EBAY FEES	TOTAL COST	PROFIT/ LOSS

STORE NAME: _____   MONTH: _____   YEAR_____

DATE	ITEM	SOLD PRICE	SHIPPING	TOTAL PRICE	COGS	SHIPPING	EBAY FEES	TOTAL COST	PROFIT/ LOSS

STORE NAME: _____ MONTH: _____ YEAR _____ EBAY DAILY SALES TRACKERS

DATE	ITEM	SOLD PRICE	SHIPPING	TOTAL PRICE	COGS	SHIPPING	EBAY FEES	TOTAL COST	PROFIT/ LOSS

STORE NAME: _____ MONTH: _____ YEAR _____

EBAY DAILY SALES TRACKERS

DATE	ITEM	SOLD PRICE	SHIPPING	TOTAL PRICE	COGS	SHIPPING	EBAY FEES	TOTAL COST	PROFIT/ LOSS

STORE NAME: _____ MONTH: _____ YEAR _____

EBAY DAILY SALES TRACKERS

DATE	ITEM	SOLD PRICE	SHIPPING	TOTAL PRICE	COGS	SHIPPING	EBAY FEES	TOTAL COST	PROFIT/ LOSS

EBAY DAILY SALES TRACKERS

STORE NAME: _____ MONTH: _____ YEAR _____

DATE	ITEM	SOLD PRICE	SHIPPING	TOTAL PRICE	COGS	SHIPPING	EBAY FEES	TOTAL COST	PROFIT/ LOSS

STORE NAME: _____ MONTH: _____ YEAR _____

EBAY DAILY SALES TRACKERS

DATE	ITEM	SOLD PRICE	SHIPPING	TOTAL PRICE	COGS	SHIPPING	EBAY FEES	TOTAL COST	PROFIT/ LOSS

STORE NAME: _____   MONTH: _____   YEAR _____

EBAY DAILY SALES TRACKERS

DATE	ITEM	SOLD PRICE	SHIPPING	TOTAL PRICE	COGS	SHIPPING	EBAY FEES	TOTAL COST	PROFIT/ LOSS

STORE NAME: _____   MONTH: _____   YEAR _____   EBAY DAILY SALES TRACKERS

DATE	ITEM	SOLD PRICE	SHIPPING	TOTAL PRICE	COGS	SHIPPING	EBAY FEES	TOTAL COST	PROFIT/ LOSS

STORE NAME: _____ MONTH: _____ YEAR _____

EBAY DAILY SALES TRACKERS

DATE	ITEM	SOLD PRICE	SHIPPING	TOTAL PRICE	COGS	SHIPPING	EBAY FEES	TOTAL COST	PROFIT/ LOSS

STORE NAME: _____ MONTH: _____ YEAR _____ EBAY DAILY SALES TRACKERS

DATE	ITEM	SOLD PRICE	SHIPPING	TOTAL PRICE	COGS	SHIPPING	EBAY FEES	TOTAL COST	PROFIT/LOSS

STORE NAME: _____ MONTH: _____ YEAR: _____

EBAY DAILY SALES TRACKERS

DATE	ITEM	SOLD PRICE	SHIPPING	TOTAL PRICE	COGS	SHIPPING	EBAY FEES	TOTAL COST	PROFIT/ LOSS

STORE NAME: _____ MONTH: _____ YEAR _____

EBAY DAILY SALES TRACKERS

DATE	ITEM	SOLD PRICE	SHIPPING	TOTAL PRICE	COGS	SHIPPING	EBAY FEES	TOTAL COST	PROFIT/ LOSS

STORE NAME: _____   MONTH: _____   YEAR _____

EBAY DAILY SALES TRACKERS

DATE	ITEM	SOLD PRICE	SHIPPING	TOTAL PRICE	COGS	SHIPPING	EBAY FEES	TOTAL COST	PROFIT/ LOSS

STORE NAME: _____ MONTH: _____ YEAR _____

DATE	ITEM	SOLD PRICE	SHIPPING	TOTAL PRICE	COGS	SHIPPING	EBAY FEES	TOTAL COST	PROFIT/LOSS

STORE NAME: _____   MONTH: _____   YEAR _____

DATE	ITEM	SOLD PRICE	SHIPPING	TOTAL PRICE	COGS	SHIPPING	EBAY FEES	TOTAL COST	PROFIT/ LOSS

STORE NAME: _____   MONTH: _____   YEAR _____

EBAY DAILY SALES TRACKERS

DATE	ITEM	SOLD PRICE	SHIPPING	TOTAL PRICE	COGS	SHIPPING	EBAY FEES	TOTAL COST	PROFIT/ LOSS

STORE NAME: _____   MONTH: _____   YEAR _____

DATE	ITEM	SOLD PRICE	SHIPPING	TOTAL PRICE	COGS	SHIPPING	EBAY FEES	TOTAL COST	PROFIT/ LOSS

STORE NAME: _____ MONTH: _____ YEAR _____

DATE	ITEM	SOLD PRICE	SHIPPING	TOTAL PRICE	COGS	SHIPPING	EBAY FEES	TOTAL COST	PROFIT/ LOSS

EBAY DAILY SALES TRACKERS

STORE NAME: _____

MONTH: _____   YEAR _____

DATE	ITEM	SOLD PRICE	SHIPPING	TOTAL PRICE	COGS	SHIPPING	EBAY FEES	TOTAL COST	PROFIT/LOSS

STORE NAME: _____   MONTH: _____   YEAR _____   EBAY DAILY SALES TRACKERS

DATE	ITEM	SOLD PRICE	SHIPPING	TOTAL PRICE	COGS	SHIPPING	EBAY FEES	TOTAL COST	PROFIT/ LOSS

STORE NAME: _____ MONTH: _____ YEAR _____

EBAY DAILY SALES TRACKERS

DATE	ITEM	SOLD PRICE	SHIPPING	TOTAL PRICE	COGS	SHIPPING	EBAY FEES	TOTAL COST	PROFIT/ LOSS

STORE NAME: _____ MONTH: _____ YEAR _____

DATE	ITEM	SOLD PRICE	SHIPPING	TOTAL PRICE	COGS	SHIPPING	EBAY FEES	TOTAL COST	PROFIT/LOSS

EBAY DAILY SALES TRACKERS

STORE NAME: _____   MONTH: _____   YEAR: _____

DATE	ITEM	SOLD PRICE	SHIPPING	TOTAL PRICE	COGS	SHIPPING	EBAY FEES	TOTAL COST	PROFIT/ LOSS

STORE NAME: _____ MONTH: _____ YEAR _____

DATE	ITEM	SOLD PRICE	SHIPPING	TOTAL PRICE	COGS	SHIPPING	EBAY FEES	TOTAL COST	PROFIT/ LOSS

EBAY DAILY SALES TRACKERS

STORE NAME: _____   MONTH: _____   YEAR _____

DATE	ITEM	SOLD PRICE	SHIPPING	TOTAL PRICE	COGS	SHIPPING	EBAY FEES	TOTAL COST	PROFIT/LOSS

STORE NAME: _____   MONTH: _____   YEAR _____

DATE	ITEM	SOLD PRICE	SHIPPING	TOTAL PRICE	COGS	SHIPPING	EBAY FEES	TOTAL COST	PROFIT/ LOSS

STORE NAME: _____   MONTH: _____   YEAR: _____

EBAY DAILY SALES TRACKERS

DATE	ITEM	SOLD PRICE	SHIPPING	TOTAL PRICE	COGS	SHIPPING	EBAY FEES	TOTAL COST	PROFIT/ LOSS

STORE NAME: _____ MONTH: _____ YEAR _____

DATE	ITEM	SOLD PRICE	SHIPPING	TOTAL PRICE	COGS	SHIPPING	EBAY FEES	TOTAL COST	PROFIT/ LOSS

STORE NAME: _____ MONTH: _____ YEAR _____

DATE	ITEM	SOLD PRICE	SHIPPING	TOTAL PRICE	COGS	SHIPPING	EBAY FEES	TOTAL COST	PROFIT/ LOSS

STORE NAME: _____ MONTH: _____ YEAR _____

DATE	ITEM	SOLD PRICE	SHIPPING	TOTAL PRICE	COGS	SHIPPING	EBAY FEES	TOTAL COST	PROFIT/ LOSS

EBAY DAILY SALES TRACKERS

STORE NAME: _____   MONTH: _____   YEAR _____

DATE	ITEM	SOLD PRICE	SHIPPING	TOTAL PRICE	COGS	SHIPPING	EBAY FEES	TOTAL COST	PROFIT/ LOSS

STORE NAME: _____ MONTH: _____ YEAR _____

EBAY DAILY SALES TRACKERS

DATE	ITEM	SOLD PRICE	SHIPPING	TOTAL PRICE	COGS	SHIPPING	EBAY FEES	TOTAL COST	PROFIT/ LOSS

EBAY DAILY SALES TRACKERS

STORE NAME: _____   MONTH: _____   YEAR _____

DATE	ITEM	SOLD PRICE	SHIPPING	TOTAL PRICE	COGS	SHIPPING	EBAY FEES	TOTAL COST	PROFIT/ LOSS

STORE NAME: _____   MONTH: _____   YEAR _____

DATE	ITEM	SOLD PRICE	SHIPPING	TOTAL PRICE	COGS	SHIPPING	EBAY FEES	TOTAL COST	PROFIT/ LOSS

EBAY DAILY SALES TRACKERS

STORE NAME: _____ MONTH: _____ YEAR _____

DATE	ITEM	SOLD PRICE	SHIPPING	TOTAL PRICE	COGS	SHIPPING	EBAY FEES	TOTAL COST	PROFIT/ LOSS

STORE NAME: _____ MONTH: _____ YEAR _____

DATE	ITEM	SOLD PRICE	SHIPPING	TOTAL PRICE	COGS	SHIPPING	EBAY FEES	TOTAL COST	PROFIT/ LOSS

STORE NAME: _____ MONTH: _____ YEAR _____

EBAY DAILY SALES TRACKERS

DATE	ITEM	SOLD PRICE	SHIPPING	TOTAL PRICE	COGS	SHIPPING	EBAY FEES	TOTAL COST	PROFIT/ LOSS

STORE NAME: _____ MONTH: _____ YEAR _____

EBAY DAILY SALES TRACKERS

DATE	ITEM	SOLD PRICE	SHIPPING	TOTAL PRICE	COGS	SHIPPING	EBAY FEES	TOTAL COST	PROFIT/ LOSS

STORE NAME: _____ MONTH: _____ YEAR _____

EBAY DAILY SALES TRACKERS

DATE	ITEM	SOLD PRICE	SHIPPING	TOTAL PRICE	COGS	SHIPPING	EBAY FEES	TOTAL COST	PROFIT/ LOSS

STORE NAME: _____ MONTH: _____ YEAR _____

EBAY DAILY SALES TRACKERS

DATE	ITEM	SOLD PRICE	SHIPPING	TOTAL PRICE	COGS	SHIPPING	EBAY FEES	TOTAL COST	PROFIT/LOSS

EBAY DAILY SALES TRACKERS

STORE NAME: _____   MONTH: _____   YEAR _____

DATE	ITEM	SOLD PRICE	SHIPPING	TOTAL PRICE	COGS	SHIPPING	EBAY FEES	TOTAL COST	PROFIT/ LOSS

STORE NAME: _____ MONTH: _____ YEAR _____

DATE	ITEM	SOLD PRICE	SHIPPING	TOTAL PRICE	COGS	SHIPPING	EBAY FEES	TOTAL COST	PROFIT/LOSS

STORE NAME: _____ MONTH: _____ YEAR _____

EBAY DAILY SALES TRACKERS

DATE	ITEM	SOLD PRICE	SHIPPING	TOTAL PRICE	COGS	SHIPPING	EBAY FEES	TOTAL COST	PROFIT/ LOSS

STORE NAME: _____   MONTH: _____   YEAR _____   EBAY DAILY SALES TRACKERS

DATE	ITEM	SOLD PRICE	SHIPPING	TOTAL PRICE	COGS	SHIPPING	EBAY FEES	TOTAL COST	PROFIT/ LOSS

EBAY DAILY SALES TRACKERS

STORE NAME: _____ MONTH: _____ YEAR _____

DATE	ITEM	SOLD PRICE	SHIPPING	TOTAL PRICE	COGS	SHIPPING	EBAY FEES	TOTAL COST	PROFIT/LOSS

STORE NAME: _____ MONTH: _____ YEAR _____

DATE	ITEM	SOLD PRICE	SHIPPING	TOTAL PRICE	COGS	SHIPPING	EBAY FEES	TOTAL COST	PROFIT/ LOSS

EBAY DAILY SALES TRACKERS

STORE NAME: _____   MONTH: _____   YEAR _____

DATE	ITEM	SOLD PRICE	SHIPPING	TOTAL PRICE	COGS	SHIPPING	EBAY FEES	TOTAL COST	PROFIT/LOSS

STORE NAME: _____   MONTH: _____   YEAR _____   EBAY DAILY SALES TRACKERS

DATE	ITEM	SOLD PRICE	SHIPPING	TOTAL PRICE	COGS	SHIPPING	EBAY FEES	TOTAL COST	PROFIT/ LOSS

STORE NAME: _____   MONTH: _____   YEAR _____

DATE	ITEM	SOLD PRICE	SHIPPING	TOTAL PRICE	COGS	SHIPPING	EBAY FEES	TOTAL COST	PROFIT/ LOSS

STORE NAME: _____   MONTH: _____   YEAR: _____   EBAY DAILY SALES TRACKERS

DATE	ITEM	SOLD PRICE	SHIPPING	TOTAL PRICE	COGS	SHIPPING	EBAY FEES	TOTAL COST	PROFIT/ LOSS

EBAY DAILY SALES TRACKERS

STORE NAME: _____ MONTH: _____ YEAR _____

DATE	ITEM	SOLD PRICE	SHIPPING	TOTAL PRICE	COGS	SHIPPING	EBAY FEES	TOTAL COST	PROFIT/ LOSS

STORE NAME: _____ MONTH: _____ YEAR _____

DATE	ITEM	SOLD PRICE	SHIPPING	TOTAL PRICE	COGS	SHIPPING	EBAY FEES	TOTAL COST	PROFIT/LOSS

EBAY DAILY SALES TRACKERS

STORE NAME: _____   MONTH: _____   YEAR _____

DATE	ITEM	SOLD PRICE	SHIPPING	TOTAL PRICE	COGS	SHIPPING	EBAY FEES	TOTAL COST	PROFIT/ LOSS

STORE NAME: _____ MONTH: _____ YEAR _____

EBAY DAILY SALES TRACKERS

DATE	ITEM	SOLD PRICE	SHIPPING	TOTAL PRICE	COGS	SHIPPING	EBAY FEES	TOTAL COST	PROFIT/ LOSS

STORE NAME: _____ MONTH: _____ YEAR _____

DATE	ITEM	SOLD PRICE	SHIPPING	TOTAL PRICE	COGS	SHIPPING	EBAY FEES	TOTAL COST	PROFIT/ LOSS

STORE NAME: _____ MONTH: _____ YEAR _____

DATE	ITEM	SOLD PRICE	SHIPPING	TOTAL PRICE	COGS	SHIPPING	EBAY FEES	TOTAL COST	PROFIT/ LOSS

STORE NAME: _____ MONTH: _____ YEAR: _____ EBAY DAILY SALES TRACKERS

DATE	ITEM	SOLD PRICE	SHIPPING	TOTAL PRICE	COGS	SHIPPING	EBAY FEES	TOTAL COST	PROFIT/ LOSS

STORE NAME: _____ MONTH: _____ YEAR _____

DATE	ITEM	SOLD PRICE	SHIPPING	TOTAL PRICE	COGS	SHIPPING	EBAY FEES	TOTAL COST	PROFIT/ LOSS

EBAY DAILY SALES TRACKERS

STORE NAME: _____   MONTH: _____   YEAR _____

DATE	ITEM	SOLD PRICE	SHIPPING	TOTAL PRICE	COGS	SHIPPING	EBAY FEES	TOTAL COST	PROFIT/ LOSS

STORE NAME: _____ MONTH: _____ YEAR _____

EBAY DAILY SALES TRACKERS

DATE	ITEM	SOLD PRICE	SHIPPING	TOTAL PRICE	COGS	SHIPPING	EBAY FEES	TOTAL COST	PROFIT/ LOSS

STORE NAME: _____ MONTH: _____ YEAR _____

EBAY DAILY SALES TRACKERS

DATE	ITEM	SOLD PRICE	SHIPPING	TOTAL PRICE	COGS	SHIPPING	EBAY FEES	TOTAL COST	PROFIT/ LOSS

STORE NAME: _____ MONTH: _____ YEAR _____

DATE	ITEM	SOLD PRICE	SHIPPING	TOTAL PRICE	COGS	SHIPPING	EBAY FEES	TOTAL COST	PROFIT/ LOSS

EBAY DAILY SALES TRACKERS

STORE NAME: _____   MONTH: _____   YEAR _____

DATE	ITEM	SOLD PRICE	SHIPPING	TOTAL PRICE	COGS	SHIPPING	EBAY FEES	TOTAL COST	PROFIT/ LOSS

STORE NAME: _____   MONTH: _____   YEAR: _____

EBAY DAILY SALES TRACKERS

DATE	ITEM	SOLD PRICE	SHIPPING	TOTAL PRICE	COGS	SHIPPING	EBAY FEES	TOTAL COST	PROFIT/ LOSS

EBAY DAILY SALES TRACKERS

STORE NAME: _____

MONTH: _____   YEAR _____

DATE	ITEM	SOLD PRICE	SHIPPING	TOTAL PRICE	COGS	SHIPPING	EBAY FEES	TOTAL COST	PROFIT/LOSS

STORE NAME: _____   MONTH: _____   YEAR _____

DATE	ITEM	SOLD PRICE	SHIPPING	TOTAL PRICE	COGS	SHIPPING	EBAY FEES	TOTAL COST	PROFIT/ LOSS

EBAY DAILY SALES TRACKERS

STORE NAME: _____   MONTH: _____   YEAR _____

DATE	ITEM	SOLD PRICE	SHIPPING	TOTAL PRICE	COGS	SHIPPING	EBAY FEES	TOTAL COST	PROFIT/ LOSS

STORE NAME: _____ MONTH: _____ YEAR _____ EBAY DAILY SALES TRACKERS

DATE	ITEM	SOLD PRICE	SHIPPING	TOTAL PRICE	COGS	SHIPPING	EBAY FEES	TOTAL COST	PROFIT/ LOSS

STORE NAME: _____ MONTH: _____ YEAR _____

EBAY DAILY SALES TRACKERS

DATE	ITEM	SOLD PRICE	SHIPPING	TOTAL PRICE	COGS	SHIPPING	EBAY FEES	TOTAL COST	PROFIT/ LOSS

STORE NAME: _____ MONTH: _____ YEAR _____

DATE	ITEM	SOLD PRICE	SHIPPING	TOTAL PRICE	COGS	SHIPPING	EBAY FEES	TOTAL COST	PROFIT/ LOSS

EBAY DAILY SALES TRACKERS

STORE NAME: _____   MONTH: _____   YEAR _____

DATE	ITEM	SOLD PRICE	SHIPPING	TOTAL PRICE	COGS	SHIPPING	EBAY FEES	TOTAL COST	PROFIT/ LOSS

STORE NAME: _____ MONTH: _____ YEAR: _____

EBAY DAILY SALES TRACKERS

DATE	ITEM	SOLD PRICE	SHIPPING	TOTAL PRICE	COGS	SHIPPING	EBAY FEES	TOTAL COST	PROFIT/ LOSS

EBAY DAILY SALES TRACKERS

STORE NAME: _____ MONTH: _____ YEAR _____

DATE	ITEM	SOLD PRICE	SHIPPING	TOTAL PRICE	COGS	SHIPPING	EBAY FEES	TOTAL COST	PROFIT/ LOSS

STORE NAME: _____ MONTH: _____ YEAR _____

EBAY DAILY SALES TRACKERS

DATE	ITEM	SOLD PRICE	SHIPPING	TOTAL PRICE	COGS	SHIPPING	EBAY FEES	TOTAL COST	PROFIT/ LOSS

STORE NAME: _____   MONTH: _____   YEAR _____

EBAY DAILY SALES TRACKERS

DATE	ITEM	SOLD PRICE	SHIPPING	TOTAL PRICE	COGS	SHIPPING	EBAY FEES	TOTAL COST	PROFIT/ LOSS

STORE NAME: _____ MONTH: _____ YEAR _____

DATE	ITEM	SOLD PRICE	SHIPPING	TOTAL PRICE	COGS	SHIPPING	EBAY FEES	TOTAL COST	PROFIT/LOSS

EBAY DAILY SALES TRACKERS

STORE NAME: _____   MONTH: _____   YEAR _____

DATE	ITEM	SOLD PRICE	SHIPPING	TOTAL PRICE	COGS	SHIPPING	EBAY FEES	TOTAL COST	PROFIT/ LOSS

STORE NAME: _____ MONTH: _____ YEAR _____

DATE	ITEM	SOLD PRICE	SHIPPING	TOTAL PRICE	COGS	SHIPPING	EBAY FEES	TOTAL COST	PROFIT/ LOSS

STORE NAME: _____ MONTH: _____ YEAR _____

DATE	ITEM	SOLD PRICE	SHIPPING	TOTAL PRICE	COGS	SHIPPING	EBAY FEES	TOTAL COST	PROFIT/ LOSS

STORE NAME: _____ MONTH: _____ YEAR _____

DATE	ITEM	SOLD PRICE	SHIPPING	TOTAL PRICE	COGS	SHIPPING	EBAY FEES	TOTAL COST	PROFIT/ LOSS

STORE NAME: _____   MONTH: _____   YEAR _____

DATE	ITEM	SOLD PRICE	SHIPPING	TOTAL PRICE	COGS	SHIPPING	EBAY FEES	TOTAL COST	PROFIT/ LOSS

STORE NAME: _____

MONTH: _____ YEAR _____

DATE	ITEM	SOLD PRICE	SHIPPING	TOTAL PRICE	COGS	SHIPPING	EBAY FEES	TOTAL COST	PROFIT/ LOSS

EBAY DAILY SALES TRACKERS

STORE NAME: _____ MONTH: _____ YEAR _____

DATE	ITEM	SOLD PRICE	SHIPPING	TOTAL PRICE	COGS	SHIPPING	EBAY FEES	TOTAL COST	PROFIT/ LOSS

STORE NAME: _____ MONTH: _____ YEAR: _____

DATE	ITEM	SOLD PRICE	SHIPPING	TOTAL PRICE	COGS	SHIPPING	EBAY FEES	TOTAL COST	PROFIT/ LOSS

EBAY DAILY SALES TRACKERS

STORE NAME: _____ MONTH: _____ YEAR _____

DATE	ITEM	SOLD PRICE	SHIPPING	TOTAL PRICE	COGS	SHIPPING	EBAY FEES	TOTAL COST	PROFIT/ LOSS

STORE NAME: _____ MONTH: _____ YEAR _____

DATE	ITEM	SOLD PRICE	SHIPPING	TOTAL PRICE	COGS	SHIPPING	EBAY FEES	TOTAL COST	PROFIT/ LOSS

STORE NAME: _____ MONTH: _____ YEAR _____ EBAY DAILY SALES TRACKERS

DATE	ITEM	SOLD PRICE	SHIPPING	TOTAL PRICE	COGS	SHIPPING	EBAY FEES	TOTAL COST	PROFIT/ LOSS

STORE NAME: _____   MONTH: _____   YEAR _____

DATE	ITEM	SOLD PRICE	SHIPPING	TOTAL PRICE	COGS	SHIPPING	EBAY FEES	TOTAL COST	PROFIT/ LOSS

STORE NAME: _____   MONTH: _____   YEAR _____   EBAY DAILY SALES TRACKERS

DATE	ITEM	SOLD PRICE	SHIPPING	TOTAL PRICE	COGS	SHIPPING	EBAY FEES	TOTAL COST	PROFIT/ LOSS

STORE NAME: _____ MONTH: _____ YEAR _____

EBAY DAILY SALES TRACKERS

DATE	ITEM	SOLD PRICE	SHIPPING	TOTAL PRICE	COGS	SHIPPING	EBAY FEES	TOTAL COST	PROFIT/ LOSS

STORE NAME: _____ MONTH: _____ YEAR _____

EBAY DAILY SALES TRACKERS

DATE	ITEM	SOLD PRICE	SHIPPING	TOTAL PRICE	COGS	SHIPPING	EBAY FEES	TOTAL COST	PROFIT/ LOSS

STORE NAME: _____   MONTH: _____   YEAR _____

EBAY DAILY SALES TRACKERS

DATE	ITEM	SOLD PRICE	SHIPPING	TOTAL PRICE	COGS	SHIPPING	EBAY FEES	TOTAL COST	PROFIT/ LOSS

STORE NAME: _____ MONTH: _____ YEAR _____

EBAY DAILY SALES TRACKERS

DATE	ITEM	SOLD PRICE	SHIPPING	TOTAL PRICE	COGS	SHIPPING	EBAY FEES	TOTAL COST	PROFIT/ LOSS

STORE NAME: _____ MONTH: _____ YEAR _____

EBAY DAILY SALES TRACKERS

DATE	ITEM	SOLD PRICE	SHIPPING	TOTAL PRICE	COGS	SHIPPING	EBAY FEES	TOTAL COST	PROFIT/ LOSS

STORE NAME: _____ MONTH: _____ YEAR _____

EBAY DAILY SALES TRACKERS

DATE	ITEM	SOLD PRICE	SHIPPING	TOTAL PRICE	COGS	SHIPPING	EBAY FEES	TOTAL COST	PROFIT/ LOSS

STORE NAME: _____ MONTH: _____ YEAR _____ EBAY DAILY SALES TRACKERS

DATE	ITEM	SOLD PRICE	SHIPPING	TOTAL PRICE	COGS	SHIPPING	EBAY FEES	TOTAL COST	PROFIT/ LOSS

STORE NAME: _____ MONTH: _____ YEAR _____ EBAY DAILY SALES TRACKERS

DATE	ITEM	SOLD PRICE	SHIPPING	TOTAL PRICE	COGS	SHIPPING	EBAY FEES	TOTAL COST	PROFIT/ LOSS

Made in United States
North Haven, CT
16 December 2021